Choose Grace

Choose Grace

3-MINUTE DEVOTIONS FOR WOMEN

BARBOUR BOOKS
An Imprint of Barbour Publishing, Inc.

Print ISBN: 978-1-68322-255-2

eBook Editions:
Adobe Digital Edition (.epub) 978-1-68322-531-7
Kindle and MobiPocket Edition (.prc) 978-1-68322-532-4

Our mission is to publish and distribute inspirational products offering exceptional value and biblical encouragement to the masses.

Member of the
Evangelical Christian
Publishers Association

Introduction

GOD is good to one and all;
everything he does is suffused with grace.

PSALM 145:9 MSG

These devotions are especially for those days when you need a bit of encouragement and a gentle reminder to: *Choose Grace!* Three minutes from your busy day is all you'll need to refresh your spirit and fill your cup to overflowing with grace for life's journey.

- Minute 1: Read and reflect on God's Word.
- Minute 2: Read the devotion and think about how it applies to your life.
- Minute 3: Pray.

Although these devotions aren't meant as tools for deep Bible study, they can be a touchstone to keep you grounded and focused on the Grace-Giver. May this book remind you that the matchless grace of the heavenly Father is woven into life's everyday moments.

Steady...

*People with their minds set on you,
you keep completely whole, steady on their feet,
because they keep at it and don't quit.*

Isaiah 26:3 MSG

One of the meanings of *grace* is "an effortless beauty of movement." A person with this kind of grace doesn't trip over her own feet; she's not clumsy or awkward, but instead she moves easily, fluidly, steadily. From a spiritual perspective, most of us stumble quite a bit—and yet we don't give up. We know that God holds our hands, and He will keep us steady even when we would otherwise fall flat on our faces.

Father, I don't always feel so graceful. Thank You for holding my hand, steadying my feet, and giving me the strength to keep at it, even when I stumble. Amen.

Life and Nourishment

*"I, the LORD, am the one who answers your
prayers and watches over you. I am like a green
pine tree; your blessings come from me."*

HOSEA 14:8 NCV

T hink of it: God is like a tree growing at the center of your
life! In the shade of this tree, you find shelter. This tree is ev-
ergreen, with deep roots that draw up life and nourishment.
Each one of life's daily blessings is the fruit of this tree. It
is the source of all your life, all your joy, and all your being.

*Lord, how can I thank You for answering my prayers and
watching over me? I am grateful for Your many blessings and
for You, the source of my being. Amen.*

Look Up!

The heavens declare the glory of God;
the skies proclaim the work of his hands.

PSALM 19:1 NIV

Grace is as near as the sky over your head. Look up and be reminded of how wonderful God truly is. The same God who created the sun and the atmosphere, the stars and the galaxies, the same God who day by day creates a new sunrise and a new sunset, that same God loves you and creates beauty in your life each day!

Father, when I look to the heavens, I am reminded that You are Creator, Giver of grace, and Author of beauty. Thank You for surrounding me with the work of Your hands. Amen.

Follow Jesus

"Whoever serves me must follow me;
and where I am, my servant also will be.
My Father will honor the one who serves me."

JOHN 12:26 NIV

A disciple is someone who follows. That is the discipline we practice: We follow Jesus. Wherever He is, we go. In His presence we find the daily grace we need to live. As we serve Him, God honors us; He affirms our dignity and makes us all we were meant to be.

Jesus, I long to be Your disciple. Give me the grace to follow You, a heart to serve You, and a mind in tune with You every minute of every day. Amen.

By His Grace

A person is made right with God
through faith, not through obeying the law.

ROMANS 3:28 NCV

Human laws can never make us into the people we are meant to be. No matter how scrupulous we try to be, we will always fall short. Our hands and hearts will come up empty. But as we fix our eyes on God, committing our lives and ourselves to Him, we are made right. We are healed and made whole by His grace, exactly as God meant us to be.

Father, rather than working to become righteous in Your sight,
help me instead to focus on increasing my faith and trusting in
Your grace. Amen.

"Extended" Family

God sets the lonely in families.

PSALM 68:6 NIV

God knows that we need others. We need their love and support, their understanding, and their simple physical presence nearby. That is why He gives us families. Families don't need to be related by blood, though. They might be the people you work with, or the people you go to church with, or the group of friends you've known since grade school. Whoever they are, they're the people who make God's grace real to you every day.

Father, thank You for creating me with a longing for connection. Thank You for those You have placed in my life to make me more of who You created me to be. Amen.

Perception

"The LORD himself goes before you and will be
with you; he will never leave you nor forsake you.
Do not be afraid; do not be discouraged."

DEUTERONOMY 31:8 NIV

The world we see with our eyes is only a piece of reality, a
glimpse into an enormous and mysterious universe. Just as
our eyes often deceive us, so do our feelings. We perceive
life through our emotions, but they are as limited as our
physical vision. Whether we sense God's presence or not,
He is always with us. Grace waits to meet us in the future, so
we can disregard all our feelings of fear and discouragement.

*Father, even though I sometimes feel alone, You remind me
that my feelings are not facts, for You are always with me.
Thank You for the peace Your presence provides. Amen.*

Daily Miracles

*"That is why I tell you not to worry about everyday life—
whether you have enough food and drink,
or enough clothes to wear. Isn't life more
than food, and your body more than clothing?"*

MATTHEW 6:25 NLT

With our eyes fixed on what we don't have, we often overlook the grace we have already received. God has blessed us
in many ways. Our bodies function day after day in amazing
ways we take for granted, and life is filled with an abundance
of daily miracles. Why do we worry so much about the details
when we live in such a vast sea of daily grace?

*Father, You are my Provider. You have promised to give me
everything I need. Help me to remember this truth and to lose
myself in the vast sea of Your amazing grace. Amen.*

Lavish and Abundant

*Let them come back to G*OD*, who is merciful,
come back to our God, who is lavish with forgiveness.*

ISAIAH 55:7 MSG

God's forgiveness is never stingy or grudging. And He never waits to offer it to us. Instead, it's always there, a lavish, abundant flood of grace, just waiting for us to turn away from our sin and accept it.

*Lord, when I am consumed by sin, my back is turned to You.
Thank You for Your mercy and lavish forgiveness that gently
turn me toward Your loving arms. Amen.*

Satisfied

Satisfy us in the morning with your unfailing love,
that we may sing for joy and be glad all our days.

PSALM 90:14 NIV

God wants to fulfill you. He wants you to feel satisfied with life so that you will catch yourself humming or singing His praises all day long. Even when life is hard, He is waiting to comfort you with His unfailing love so that gladness will creep over your heart once more.

Father, You are the Author of joy. Thank You so much for Your unfailing love that fills me to the brim. Give me grace and gladness every minute of every day. Amen.

Safe

*My life is in your hands. Save me from my enemies
and from those who are chasing me.*

PSALM 31:15 NCV

Do you ever feel like trouble is chasing you? No matter how fast you run or how you try to hide, it comes relentlessly after you, dogging your footsteps, breathing its hot breath down your neck, robbing you of peace. What's even worse is that it waits for you down the road as well! Maybe you need to stop running and hiding and instead let yourself drop into God's hands, knowing He will hold your future safe.

---

*Lord, when I am afraid, my instinct is to run. Thank You
for this reminder that my life is in Your hands.
Keep me safe. Help me to be still. Amen.*

Happiness Requirement. . .

I'm just as happy with little as with much, with much as with little. . . .Whatever I have, wherever I am, I can make it through anything in the One who makes me who I am.

PHILIPPIANS 4:12 MSG

When you were younger, what did you think you needed to be happy? Nice clothes? A boyfriend? A husband? A good job? At the point where you are in your life now, what is it you think your happiness requires? Day after day, God blesses us, but our happiness does not depend on those blessings. Our joy depends only on God. When we realize that, we no longer have to worry about losing or gaining life's blessings.

Jesus, Giver of joy, help me to learn the secret of contentment. Help me to rest in the assurance that whatever life gives or takes away, I can always depend on You. Amen.

Whole and Healthy

When Jesus heard this, he told them, "Healthy people don't
need a doctor—sick people do. I have come to call not
those who think they are righteous, but those
who know they are sinners."

MARK 2:17 NLT

With Jesus, we never need to pretend to be something
we aren't. We don't need to impress Him with our spiritual
maturity and mental acuity. Instead, we can come to Him
honestly, with all our neediness, admitting just how weak
we are. When we do, we let down the barriers that keep
Him out of our hearts. We allow His grace to make us whole
and healthy.

*Jesus, help me to resist the temptation to be something
I'm not. Instead, give me a spirit of vulnerability
so that I can receive Your healing grace. Amen.*

Spirit-Oxygen

Tell me this one thing: How did you receive the Holy Spirit?
Did you receive the Spirit by following the law?
No, you received the Spirit because you
heard the Good News and believed it.

GALATIANS 3:2 NCV

As we share the good news of Christ, we need to take care that we are not preaching the law rather than the love of Christ. The Spirit did not come into your heart through legalism and laws—and He won't reach others through you if that is your focus. Breathe deeply of grace, and let it spread from you to a world that is desperate for the oxygen of the Spirit.

Father, Son, and Holy Spirit, how grateful I am for the good
news of the Gospel. Remind me of the grace I have received,
and enable me to share it freely with others. Amen.

Unchanged

Why am I discouraged? Why is my heart so sad?
I will put my hope in God!
PSALM 42:5 NLT

Thousands of years ago, the psalmist who wrote these words expressed the same feelings we all have. Some days we just feel blue. The world looks dark, everything seems to be going wrong, and our hearts are sad. Those feelings are part of the human condition. Like the psalmist, we need to remind ourselves that God is unchanged by cloudy skies and gloomy hearts. His grace is always the same, as bright and hopeful as ever.

Heavenly Father, when I am overcome by sadness,
help me to see Your light shimmering just beyond the
clouds. Thank You for Your grace, which is a bright
promise and a great comfort. Amen.

Grace of Hospitality

When God's people are in need, be ready to help them.
Always be eager to practice hospitality.

ROMANS 12:13 NLT

God opens Himself to you, offering you everything He has, and He calls you to do the same for others. Just as He made you welcome, make others welcome in your life. Don't reach out to others grudgingly, with a sense of obligation. Instead, be eager for opportunities to practice the grace of hospitality.

Father, although I long to help others in need, I can sure find a lot of excuses to avoid practicing hospitality. Please give me an eagerness to share with others. Amen.

Thinking Habits

And now, dear brothers and sisters, one final thing.
Fix your thoughts on what is true, and honorable,
and right, and pure, and lovely, and admirable.
Think about things that are excellent and worthy of praise.

PHILIPPIANS 4:8 NLT

Our brains are gifts from God, intended to serve us well, special gifts of grace we often take for granted. In return, we need to offer our minds back to God. Practice thinking positive thoughts. Focus on what is true rather than on lies; pay attention to beautiful things and stop staring at the ugly things in life. Discipline your minds to take on God's habits of thinking.

Heavenly Father, thank You for my brain, a gift from
You. Help me focus on things that honor You. Open my
eyes to beautiful, positive things—and most
importantly to Your Truth. Amen.

Into God's Presence

"That person can pray to God and find favor with him,
they will see God's face and shout for joy."

JOB 33:26 NIV

Prayer is the channel through which God's grace flows. We do not pray because God needs us to pray; we pray because we need to pray. When we come into God's presence, we are renewed. Our hearts lift. We look into the face of the One who loves us most, and we are filled with joy.

Father, thank You for the gift of prayer and the promise
that I can talk with You at any time. As I look to
You, fill my heart with Your joy. Amen.

What God Shows Us

The LORD is righteous in everything he does;
he is filled with kindness.

PSALM 145:17 NLT

Did you know that the word *kind* comes from the same root as *kin*? Both words originally had to do with intimate shared relationships like the ones that exist between members of the same family. This is what God shows us: the kindness of a good father, the gentleness of a good mother, the understanding of a brother or sister.

Good Father, thank You for Your kindness and for creating
me with a longing to be close to You. May I find
rest in Your nearness. Amen.

Laugh Out Loud

*"He will once again fill your mouth with laughter
and your lips with shouts of joy."*

JOB 8:21 NLT

Did you know that God wants to make you laugh? He wants
to fill you with loud, rowdy joy. Oh, some days His grace will
come to you quietly and calmly. But every now and then, you
will have days when He makes you laugh out loud.

*Heavenly Father, the gift of laughter is such a blessing.
Help me to look for reasons to laugh out
loud with Your joy. Amen.*

Sing!

*But each day the LORD pours his unfailing love upon me,
and through each night I sing his songs,
praying to God who gives me life.*

PSALM 42:8 NLT

Life itself is a gift of grace. The very blood that flows through our veins, the beat of our hearts, and the steady hum of our metabolism—all of that is God's free gift to us, a token of His constant and unconditional love. When we are so richly loved, how can we help but sing, even in the darkness?

*Dear Lord, Giver of blessing, Giver of life, as I experience
Your unfailing love each and every day, teach my
heart to sing Your joyful song. Amen.*

Web of Love

So now I am giving you a new commandment: Love each other.
Just as I have loved you, you should love each other.

JOHN 13:34 NLT

God's grace comes to us through a net of relationships and connections. Because we know we are totally and unconditionally loved, we can in turn love others. The connections between us grow ever wider and stronger, a web of love that unites us all with God.

Jesus, I am grateful for the relationships You have given me.
Thank You for Your love that enables me to
love and be loved by others. Amen.

Thrive!

Those who trust in their riches will fall,
but the righteous will thrive like a green leaf.

PROVERBS 11:28 NIV

Money seems so important in our world. Many things we want depend on money—that remodeling project we're hoping to do, the Christmas gifts we want to give, the vacation we hope to take, and the new car we want to drive. There's nothing wrong with any of those things, but our enjoyment of them will always be fleeting. Only God's daily grace makes us truly grow and thrive.

Father, remind me that while caring for my family,
making money, and preparing for my future are good
things, they are not my identity. Help me to
find my purpose, my worth, in You. Amen.

Sharing Life

But if we walk in the light, God himself being the light,
we also experience a shared life with one another.

1 JOHN 1:7 MSG

Some of us are extroverts, and some of us are introverts.
But either way, God asks us to share our lives in some way
with others. As we walk in His light, He gives us grace to
experience a new kind of a life, a life we have in common
with the others who share His kingdom.

Lord Jesus, I recognize that You have asked me to share my
life with others. Help me to look for opportunities to
make connections as I walk in Your light. Amen.

Healed Past

*"All their past sins will be forgotten, and they will live
because of the righteous things they have done."*

EZEKIEL 18:22 NLT

We have the feeling that we can't do anything about the
past. We think all our mistakes are back there behind us,
carved in stone. But God's creative power is amazing, and His
grace can heal even the past. Yesterday's sins are pulled out
like weeds, while the good things we have done are watered
so that they grow and flourish into the present. Give your
past to God. His grace is big enough to bring healing even
to your worst memories.

*Father, how grateful I am that my past is forgiven and that
I am free! Help me to continue to trust You to continue
to bring righteousness into my life. Amen.*

Valuable

Better to be patient than powerful;
better to have self-control than to conquer a city.

PROVERBS 16:32 NLT

Our world values visible power. We appreciate things like prestige and skill, wealth and influence. But God looks at things differently. From His perspective, the quiet, easily overlooked quality of patience is far more valuable than any worldly power. Patience makes room for others' needs and brokenness. Patience creates a space in our lives for God's grace to flow through us.

Lord, when I come to Your Word, I am constantly reminded
that Your wisdom is not the world's wisdom. Give me Your
perspective. Draw me toward the practice of patience. Amen.

Peaceful Hearts

You will keep in perfect peace all who trust in you,
all whose thoughts are fixed on you!

ISAIAH 26:3 NLT

Peace seems very far away sometimes. But it's not! Peace isn't an emotion we can work up in our own strength. It's one of the gifts of grace God longs to give us. All we need to do is focus on Him. As we give Him all our worries, one by one, every day, He will do His part: He will keep our hearts at peace.

Jesus, I am incredibly grateful for Your peace. It is a gift
I need every moment of every day. When my heart gets
anxious, comfort me with the peace only
You can provide. Amen.

An All-the-Time Thing!

*Pray diligently. Stay alert,
with your eyes wide open in gratitude.*

COLOSSIANS 4:2 MSG

Prayer is not a sometimes thing. It's an all-the-time thing! We need to pray every day, being careful to keep the lines of communication open between God and ourselves all through the day, moment by moment. When we make prayer a habit, we won't miss the many gifts of grace that come our way. And we won't forget to notice when God answers our prayers.

*Father, although it's important to set aside specific time
for prayer, I am reminded of the value of being in
constant communication with You—
my good Father, my companion. Amen.*

Right Now

*For God says, "At just the right time, I heard you. On the day
of salvation, I helped you." Indeed, the "right time"
is now. Today is the day of salvation.*

2 Corinthians 6:2 nlt

God always meets us right now, in the present moment.
We don't need to waste our time looking over our shoulders
at the past, and we don't have to feel as though we need to
reach some future moment before we can truly touch God.
He is here now. Today, this very moment, is full of His grace.

*Lord, make me mindful of Your presence right now,
in this very minute. You have redeemed my past,
and You hold my future in Your hands.
This moment is the one I must cling to. Amen.*

A Quiet Pace

"Teach me, and I will be quiet.
Show me where I have been wrong."

JOB 6:24 NCV

Do you ever feel as though you simply can't sit still? That
your thoughts are swirling so fast that you can't stop them?
That you're so busy, so stressed, so hurried that you have to
run, run, run? Take a breath. Open your heart to God. Allow
Him to quiet your frantic mind. Ask Him to show you how
you can begin again, this time walking to the quiet pace of
His grace.

Father, quietness does not always come easily.
The frenetic pace of this world sucks me in. Fill my lungs
with Your breath. Quiet me and help me to be still. Amen.

Because of Christ

*All this comes from the God who settled the relationship
between us and him, and then called us to settle
our relationships with each other.*

2 Corinthians 5:18 msg

God created a bridge to span the distance between ourselves and Him. That bridge is Christ, the best and fullest expression of divine grace. Because of Christ, we are in a relationship with the Creator of the entire world. And because of Christ, we are called to build bridges of our own, to span the distance between ourselves and others.

---

*Jesus, there is no way I could bridge the chasm between
God and myself. Your sacrifice draws me near to the Father.
May my life be a reflection of my gratitude. Amen.*

From the Inside Out

Take on an entirely new way of life—a God-fashioned life,
a life renewed from the inside and working itself into your
conduct as God accurately reproduces his character in you.

EPHESIANS 4:24 MSG

At the end of a long week, we sometimes feel tired and drained. We need to use feelings like that as wake-up calls, reminders that we need to open ourselves anew to God's Spirit so that He can renew us from the inside out. Grace has the power to change our hearts and minds, filling us with new energy to follow Jesus.

Lord, the world says change comes from the outside.
Your Word says that true transformation comes
from the inside. Meet me there—on the
inside—and make me like You. Amen.

Take a Break

"Only in returning to me and resting in me will you be saved."
Isaiah 30:15 NLT

Some days you try everything you can think of to save yourself, but no matter how hard you try, you fail again and again. You fall on your face and embarrass yourself. You hurt the people around you. You make mistakes, and nothing whatsoever seems to go right. When that happens, it's time to take a break. You need to stop trying so hard. Throw yourself in God's arms. Rest on His grace, knowing that He will save you.

Father, sometimes I feel so unsure of myself. Help me to relax, to rest in Your arms, and to remember that You are my good teacher, my support, and my comfort. Amen.

Welcome Interruptions

So they left by boat for a quiet place,
where they could be alone.

MARK 6:32 NLT

Jesus and the disciples sought a quiet place, away from the crowds. Like us, they needed alone time. But as so often happens, people interrupt those moments of solitude. The crowd follows us, the phone rings, someone comes to the door. When that happens, we must ask Jesus for the grace to follow His example and let go of our quiet moments alone, welcoming the interruption with patience and love.

Jesus, I am good at setting my own agenda. Help me to see
life's interruptions as gifts from You, rather than
disruptions to my "perfect" plan. Amen.

Praise Him!

The Lord is my strength, my song, and my salvation.
He is my God, and I will praise him.

EXODUS 15:2 TLB

God makes you strong, He makes you sing with gladness, and He rescues you from sin. These are the gifts of His grace. When He has given you so much, don't you want to give back to Him? Use your strength, your joy, and your freedom to praise Him.

Father, Your Word tells me that You have armed me
with strength! This is such a gift. Help me to use
this strength to honor You. Amen.

Where Credit Is Due

It is not that we think we are qualified to do anything on our own. Our qualification comes from God.

2 CORINTHIANS 3:5 NLT

It's easy to seek God when we feel like failures, but when success comes our way, we like to congratulate ourselves rather than give God the credit. When we achieve great things, we need to remember that it is God's grace through us that brought about our success.

Father, every good thing I do comes from You. Thank You for allowing me to collaborate with You to do Your work. It is an honor to be used by You. Amen.

Vehicle for God's Grace

Do not neglect your gift. . . . Be diligent in these matters;
give yourself wholly to them, so that everyone
may see your progress.

1 Timothy 4:14–15 niv

God expects us to use the talents He gave us. Don't turn
away from them with a false sense of modesty. Exercise them.
Improve your skills. Whatever your gift may be, use it as a
vehicle for God's grace.

Lord, help me not to bury my talents. Give me courage and
boldness to use the gifts You have given me, knowing the
more I use them, the stronger my gifts will be. Amen.

Outside of Time's Stream

Your throne, O Lord, has stood from time immemorial.
You yourself are from the everlasting past.

PSALM 93:2 NLT

If you think of time as a fast-moving river, then we are creatures caught in its stream. Life keeps slipping away from us like water between our fingers. But God is outside of time's stream. He holds our past safely in His hands, and His grace is permanent and unshakable. His love is the lifesaver to which we cling in the midst of time's wild waves.

God, when I try to understand words like immemorial
and everlasting, I am in awe. I cannot begin to
comprehend Your bigness. Give me Your
perspective. Help me to trust You. Amen.

Adorned with Grace

Don't ever forget kindness and truth.
Wear them like a necklace.

PROVERBS 3:3 NCV

Kindness and truth are strands of the same necklace. You should not be so kind that you evade the truth, nor should you be so truthful that you wound others. Instead, adorn yourself with both strands of this necklace. Wear it with grace.

Father, there exists such a perfect balance between kindness and truth. One without the other would not be enough. Give me grace to be kind and boldness to be truthful. Amen.

The Missing Pieces

Trust the LORD with all your heart,
and don't depend on your own understanding.

PROVERBS 3:5 NCV

Life is confusing. No matter how hard we try, we can't always make sense of it. We don't like it when that happens, and so we keep trying to determine what's going on, as though we were trying puzzle pieces to fill in a picture we long to see. Sometimes, though, we have to accept that in this life we will never be able to see the entire image. We have to trust God's grace for the missing pieces.

Dear Lord, my own understanding is awfully limited,
and yet I still sometimes try to depend on it.
Help me to trust You with 100 percent of my heart. Amen.

First Priorities

For Wisdom is better than all the trappings of wealth;
nothing you could wish for holds a candle to her.

PROVERBS 8:11 MSG

W hat do you value most? You may know the answer you
are "supposed" to give to that question, but you can tell the
real answer by where your time and energy are focused.
Do you spend most of your time working for and thinking
about money and physical wealth, or do you make wisdom
and grace your first priorities?

Father, if I compare myself too much with others, I can easily
get caught in the trappings of wealth. Instead, turn my focus
to You and help me to make wisdom my goal. Amen.

Wise Enough to Lead

*"To God belong wisdom and power;
counsel and understanding are his."*

JOB 12:13 NIV

The word *wisdom* comes from the same root words that have to do with vision, the ability to see into a deeper spiritual reality. Where else can we turn for the grace to see beneath life's surface except to God? Who else can we trust to be strong enough and wise enough to lead us to our eternal home?

*Lord, my vision is far from 20/20. Help me see the world
through Your lens of wisdom. Bestow on me Your counsel,
and fill me with Your understanding. Amen.*

Control

Put GOD in charge of your work,
then what you've planned will take place.

PROVERBS 16:3 MSG

Ifwe're doing a job that is important to us, it is hard to let go of our control. Not only do we hate to trust someone else to take over, but we often don't want to trust God to take charge either. We want to do it all by ourselves. But the best-laid plans fall into nothing without God's help. What's more, as we rely on His grace, we no longer need to feel stressed or pressured! We can let Him take charge.

God, the more I entrust my plans to You, the more successful
they will be. Give me the courage to trust and the
grace to rest in Your promise. Amen.

Ever Wider

A longing fulfilled is a tree of life.

PROVERBS 13:12 NIV

Take stock of your life. What were you most hoping to achieve a year ago? (Or five years ago?) How many of those goals have been achieved? Sometimes, once we've reached a goal, we move on too quickly to the next one, never allowing ourselves to find the grace God wants to reveal within that achievement. With each goal reached, His grace spreads out into your life, like a tree whose branches grow ever wider.

God, help me to find the balance between moving forward and looking back. Give me moments to pause and reflect on how far I have come with Your grace. Amen.

Christ-Balance

Jesus caught them off balance with his own test question:
"What do you think about the Christ? Whose son is he?"

MATTHEW 22:41 MSG

Sometimes Christ asks us to find new ways of thinking. . .
new ways of living. . .new ways of encountering Him in the
world around us. That is not always easy. We don't like to
be caught off balance. When our life's equilibrium is shaken,
we feel anxious, out of control. But if we rely on Christ, He
will pick us up, dust us off, and give us the grace to find our
balance in Him.

Dear Jesus, sometimes I think I have things all figured out,
and then You ask a hard question. When I am thrown
off balance, steady me with Your truth. Amen.

True Beauty

*What matters is not your outer appearance—the styling of
your hair, the jewelry you wear, the cut of your clothes—
but your inner disposition. Cultivate inner beauty,
the gentle, gracious kind that God delights in.*

1 PETER 3:3–4 MSG

We want to be beautiful. It's a longing that has been in our
hearts since we were little girls. As grown-up women, we can
become overly worried about our appearance, fretting over
whether we measure up to the demanding standards of that
little girl who still lives in our hearts. We need to relax in the
assurance of God's grace within us. As we allow His Spirit
to shine through us, we will find our deepest, truest beauty.

*God, instead of focusing on the image I see in my mirror,
help me to look into Your eyes for an accurate reflection
of the beauty You have instilled in me. Amen.*

New Insight

Your word is a lamp to guide my feet and a light for my path.
PSALM 119:105 NLT

We sometimes take the Scriptures for granted. These ancient words, though, continue to shine with light just as they did centuries ago. In them, God's grace is revealed to us. In them, we gain new insight into ourselves and our lives.

Father, every time I open Your Word, I am blessed by a fresh revelation of Your truth. May Your ancient words drip like sweet honey into the depths of my soul. Amen.

Just What We Need

God can pour on the blessings in astonishing ways
so that you're ready for anything and everything,
more than just ready to do what needs to be done.

2 CORINTHIANS 9:8 MSG

Blessings are God's grace visible to us in tangible form. Sometimes they are so small we nearly overlook them— the sun on our faces, the smile of a friend, or food on the table—but other times they amaze us. Day by day, God's grace makes us ready for whatever comes our way. He gives us exactly what we need.

God, the more I see Your blessings, the more they seem
to pour out on me. Give me Your grace to receive
and eyes to see Your goodness. Amen.

A Gift

Don't you see that children are GOD's best gift?
PSALM 127:3 MSG

W hether we have children of our own or enjoy others' children, God's grace is revealed to us in a special way through these small people. In children, we catch a glimpse of what God intended for us all, before we grew up and let life cloud our hearts. Children's hope gives us grown-ups hope as well. Their laughter makes us smile, and their love reminds us that we, too, are loved by God.

Father, thank You for the joy that children bring and
the beautiful illustration of Your love for us.
Thank You for the life lessons little ones
have to teach us. Amen.

Beautiful World

"Walk out into the fields and look at the wildflowers."
MATTHEW 6:28 MSG

Take the time to go outdoors. Look at nature. You don't have to spend hours to realize how beautiful God made the world. A single flower, if you really look at it, could be enough to fill you with awe. Sometimes we only need something very simple to remind us of God's grace.

Creator, Father, I am amazed by Your creation and the goodness reflected in its beauty. Help me to take time to enjoy this gift, to be filled to the brim with gratitude. Amen.

Law of Love

I pondered the direction of my life,
and I turned to follow your laws.

PSALM 119:59 NLT

Did you know that the word *law* comes from root words that mean "foundation" or "something firm and fixed"? Sometimes we can't help but feel confused and uncertain. When that happens, turn to God's law, His rule for living. Love is His law, the foundation that always holds firm. When we cling to that, we find direction.

Lord, when I ponder the direction of my life without Your Spirit, I am lost and uncertain. Thank You for Your Word that anchors me in truth and provides the guidance I need. Amen.

Leading

But since we belong to the day, let us be sober,
putting on faith and love as a breastplate,
and the hope of salvation as a helmet.

1 Thessalonians 5:8 niv

We sometimes think of discipline as a negative thing, as something that asks us to sacrifice and punish ourselves. But really the word has more to do with the grace we receive from instruction and learning, from following a master. Like an athlete who follows her coach's leading, we are called to follow our Master, wearing His uniform of love and His helmet of hope.

Heavenly Father, You are my Master, my Guide,
my Coach, my everything. Thank You for Your grace
and for giving me the tools I need to be self-controlled,
faithful, loving, and hopeful. Amen.

Reach Out to Him

> *"Your words have supported those who were falling;*
> *you encouraged those with shaky knees."*
>
> JOB 4:4 NLT

God knows how weak and shaky we feel some days. He understands our feelings. After all, He made us, so He understands how prone humans are to discouragement. He doesn't blame us for being human, but He never leaves us helpless, either. His grace is always there, like a hand held out to us, simply waiting for us to reach out and grasp it.

Lord, thank You for Your words that give me support and hope
when I am falling; thank You for encouraging me when
I feel shaky. May I rest in Your grace and truth. Amen.

Heartfelt

For we live by believing and not by seeing.

2 CORINTHIANS 5:7 NLT

The world of science tells us that only what can be seen and measured is truly real. But our hearts know differently. Every day, we depend on the things we believe—our faith in God and in our friends and family, our commitment to give ourselves to God and others—and it is these invisible beliefs that give us grace to live.

Father, my mind is so prone to cling to what is tangible. However, my heart is sure that You are as real as the bright shining sun. Fill me with confidence and trust. Amen.

Sticking Together

Families stick together in all kinds of trouble.

PROVERBS 17:17 MSG

Families can drive you crazy. Whether it's the people with whom you share a house or the extended family that gets together at holidays and birthdays, family members can be exasperating, even infuriating. When it comes right down to it, though, your family members are the ones who show you God's grace even when life is hard, the ones who stick by you no matter what (even when they make you crazy!).

Heavenly Father, thank You for my family. Thank You for opportunities to give and receive Your grace. When I am exasperated, remind me of the patience You have with me. Amen.

Sensitivity

At the same time, don't be callous in your exercise of freedom,
thoughtlessly stepping on the toes of those who aren't as free
as you are. I try my best to be considerate of everyone's
feelings in all these matters; I hope you will be, too.

1 CORINTHIANS 10:32–33 MSG

The person who walks in grace doesn't trip over other people's feet. She doesn't shove her way through life like a bull in a china shop. Instead, she allows the grace she has so freely received to make her more aware of others' feelings. With God-given empathy, she is sensitive to those around her, sharing the grace she has received with all she meets.

Jesus, I am grateful for the freedom I have in You. Help me to
see past my differences with others so that I can show them
empathy from a gracious and compassionate heart. Amen.

True Nourishment

He gives food to every living thing.
His faithful love endures forever.

PSALM 136:25 NLT

People often have a confused relationship with food. We love to eat, but we feel guilty when we do. We sometimes turn to food when we're tense or worried, trying to fill the empty, anxious holes in our hearts. But God wants to give us the true nourishment we need, body and soul, if only we will let Him.

Heavenly Father, any of Your good gifts used for the
wrong reasons or in excess have the potential to harm me.
Help me to have a healthy relationship with food. Amen.

God's Honor

For the honor of your name, O LORD,
forgive my many, many sins.

PSALM 25:11 NLT

Like all gifts of grace, forgiveness by its very definition is something that can never be earned. Forgiveness is what God gives us when we deserve nothing but anger. He forgives us not because we merit it, but because of His own honor. Over and over, we will turn away from God—but over and over, He will bring us back. That is who He is!

Father, I am grateful for Your unending gift of forgiveness.
Help me to relish in the joy of knowing that You always have
and always will continue to forgive my many sins. Amen.

Unconditional Grace

A friend loves at all times.

PROVERBS 17:17 NASB

Friends are the people you can allow to see you at your worst. They're the ones who can see you without your makeup. . .or walk in when your house is a mess. . .or overhear you acting like a thirteen-year-old—and they'll still be your friends. They reveal to you God's unconditional grace.

Dear Lord, thank You for my friends and the joy we share.
Thank You for their love for me—even on my worst days.
Help me to be a true and loving friend. Amen.

What You Crave

Take delight in the LORD,
and he will give you your heart's desires.
PSALM 37:4 NLT

Do you ever feel as though God wants to deny you what you want, as though He's a cruel stepparent who takes pleasure in thwarting you? That image of God is a lie. He's the One who placed your heart's desires deep inside you. As you turn to Him, knowing that He alone is the source of all true delight, He will grant you what your heart most truly craves.

Father, I cannot imagine that You love me so much that
You would reach out and give me the things my heart
desires. Yet Your Word is truth. Thank You. Amen.

Wonderful Plans

"For I know the plans I have for you," says the LORD.
"They are plans for good and not for disaster,
to give you a future and a hope."

JEREMIAH 29:11 NLT

Don't worry about the future. No matter how frightening it may look to you sometimes, God is waiting there for you. He has plans for you, wonderful plans that will lead you deeper and deeper into His grace and love.

Lord, help me never to waver in the belief that You have good plans for me. When I feel I'm falling headlong into disaster, remind me of my stable future and steady hope. Amen.

Simply Happy

Are any of you happy? You should sing praises.

JAMES 5:13 NLT

Some days are simply happy days. The sun shines, people make us laugh, and life seems good. A day like that is a special grace. Thank God for it. As you hum through your day, don't forget to sing His praises.

Father, thank You for the gift of happiness and for life in the Holy Spirit that allows me to sing praises through my days. I praise You with all my heart. Amen.

For Eternity

My health may fail, and my spirit may grow weak,
but God remains the strength of my heart;
he is mine forever.

PSALM 73:26 NLT

Sooner or later, our bodies let us down. Even the healthiest of us will one day have to face old age. When our bodies' strength fails us, we may feel discouraged and depressed. But even then we can find joy and strength in our God. When our hearts belong to the Creator of the Universe, we realize we are far more than our bodies. Because of God's unfailing grace, we will be truly healthy for all eternity.

God, when I feel discouraged by aches and pains that bring me
down, help me to remember that my life here on earth
is barely a breath in the scope of eternity. Amen.

Free!

For the Lord is the Spirit,
and wherever the Spirit of the Lord is,
there is freedom.

2 Corinthians 3:17 NLT

How do you know when the Holy Spirit is present in your life? You should be able to tell by the sense of freedom you feel. If you feel oppressed, obsessed, or depressed, something in your life is out of kilter. Seek out God's Spirit. He wants you to be free.

Holy Spirit, fill me with a sense of freedom only You
can provide. Free my spirit from chains of oppression,
and draw me into the wide open spaces of Your peace. Amen.

A Lovely Place

How lovely is your dwelling place, LORD Almighty!
PSALM 84:1 NIV

Imagine this: God considers your heart His home! It's the place where He dwells. And as a result, your heart is a lovely place, filled with the grace of the almighty God.

O Lord Almighty, I humbly invite You into my heart's home. Fill it with Your loveliness so that I can experience the comfort of Your presence and Your peace. Amen.

Amazing Expectations

Listen to my voice in the morning, LORD.
Each morning I bring my requests to
you and wait expectantly.

PSALM 5:3 NLT

You need to get in the habit of hoping. Instead of getting up in the morning and sighing as you face another dreary day, practice saying hello to God as soon as you wake up. Listen for what He wants to say to your heart. Expect Him to do amazing things each day.

Good morning, Lord. I can easily forget how necessary it is to begin my day in sweet communion with You. Tune my heart's ear to the lovely sound of Your voice. Amen.

Open Homes

Be quick to give a meal to the hungry,
a bed to the homeless—cheerfully.

1 Peter 4:9 msg

Because our homes are our private places, the places we retreat to when we're tired to find new strength, it's hard sometimes to open our homes to others. It's bad enough that we have to cope with others' needs all day long, we feel, without having to bring them home with us! But God calls us to offer our hospitality, and He will give us the grace to do it joyfully.

God, You have blessed me with a home—a sanctuary.
And I am so grateful for it. Help me to joyfully
share that blessing with others. Amen.

Beyond Intelligence

The fastest runner does not always win the race, the strongest soldier does not always win the battle, the wisest does not always have food. . . Time and chance happen to everyone.

ECCLESIASTES 9:11 NCV

How smart do you think you are? Do you assume you will be able to think your way through life's problems? Many of us do—but God reminds us that some things are beyond the scope of our intelligence. Some days life simply doesn't make sense. But even then, grace is there with us in the chaos. When we can find no rational answers to life's dilemmas, we have no choice but to rely absolutely on God.

God, I am conditioned to rely on strength, speed, and efficiency. While those things are useful, I know that wisdom is more important. Help me to seek answers directly from You. Amen.

Open to Joy

"The joy of the LORD is your strength."

NEHEMIAH 8:10 NIV

Our God is a God of joy. He is not a God of sighing and gloom. Open yourself to His joy. It is a gift of grace He longs to give you. He knows it will make you strong.

Oh Lord, Giver of joy and Source of my strength,
thank You for these gifts, which are mine in abundance.
Help me to rely on Your joy and strength. Amen.

Rope of Love

*"I led them with cords of human kindness,
with ropes of love. I lifted the yoke from their
neck and bent down and fed them."*

HOSEA 11:4 NCV

God's grace is not a lasso looped around our shoulders, trapping us and binding us tight. Instead, grace reaches out to us through the kindness of others. It is a rope of love that stretches through our lives, leading us to freedom.

*Father, Your Word contains story after story of humans
freed from bondage. I cannot begin to thank You for
the grace that frees me and allows me to thrive. Amen.*

Transformed

And Sarah declared, "God has brought me laughter.
All who hear about this will laugh with me."

GENESIS 21:6 NLT

The first time we read of Sarah laughing, it was because she
doubted God. She didn't believe that at her age she would
have a baby. But God didn't hold her laughter against her.
Instead, He transformed it. He turned her laughter of scorn
and doubt into the laughter of fulfillment and grace.

Father Redeemer, thank You for taking my very worst
moments and transforming them into a story You can
use for Your purpose and Your glory. Amen.

Full!

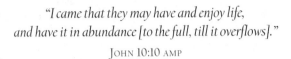

"*I came that they may have and enjoy life,
and have it in abundance [to the full, till it overflows].*"

JOHN 10:10 AMP

The life we have in Christ is not restricted or narrow. Grace doesn't flow to us in a meager trickle; it fills our life to the fullest. God's grace comes to us each moment, day after day, year after year, a generous flood that fills every crack and crevice of our lives—and then overflows.

*Jesus, I sometimes long so deeply for heaven that I forget
You have big plans for me on this earth. Thank You that
those plans involve a rich and abundant life. Amen.*

Love Is Bigger

"Love the LORD *your God with all your heart
and with all your soul and with all your might."*

DEUTERONOMY 6:5 NASB

Love is not merely a feeling. It's far bigger than that. Love fills up our emotions, but it also fills our thoughts. Our body's strength and energy feed it. It requires discipline and determination. Loving God requires the effort of our whole being.

*Oh Lord, help me to learn to love You with all my heart,
all my soul, and all my might. Give me the discipline
and determination I need to love You fiercely. Amen.*

Ten Percent

The earth is the LORD's, and everything in it.
PSALM 24:1 NLT

Do you tithe? Giving 10 percent of your income specifically to God's work is a good discipline. But sometimes we act as though that 10 percent is God's and the other 90 percent is ours. We forget that everything is God's. Through grace, He shares all of creation with us. When we look at it that way, our 10 percent tithe seems a little stingy!

Heavenly Father, everything belongs to You—even the cattle on a thousand hills. Thank You for sharing Your wealth with me, and help me to share it lavishly with others. Amen.

Loving Support

*Let us think of ways to motivate one another
to acts of love and good works.*

HEBREWS 10:24 NLT

Imagine that you're sitting in the bleachers watching one of your favorite young people play a sport. You jump up and cheer for him. You make sure he knows you're there, shouting out encouragement. Hearing your voice, he jumps higher, runs faster. That is the sort of excitement and support we need to show others around us. When we do all we can to encourage each other, love and good deeds will burst from us all.

*Lord, help me to be a cheerleader for others. Help me to see
the world through their eyes and to say and do the things
I know would motivate and encourage them. Amen.*

Looking Forward

I focus on this one thing: Forgetting the past
and looking forward to what lies ahead.

PHILIPPIANS 3:13 NLT

As followers of Christ, we are people who look forward rather than backward. We have all made mistakes, but God does not want us to dwell on them, wallowing in guilt and discouragement. Instead, He calls us to let go of the past, trusting Him to deal with it. His grace is new every moment.

Father, I sometimes ruminate over past mistakes.
Help me not to wallow in the past—instead, enable me to
delight in Your grace, which is new each moment. Amen.

Quiet Time

---

*Be still before the L*ORD*, and wait patiently for him.*

PSALM 37:7 NRSV

Our lives are busy. Responsibilities crowd our days, and at night as we go to bed, our minds often continue to be preoccupied with the day's work, ticking off a mental to-do list even as we fall asleep. We need to set aside time to quiet our hearts. In those moments, we can let go of all our to-dos and wait for God's grace to take action in our lives.

God, thank You for this verse that reminds me of the
gift of stillness. In my all-too-few quiet moments,
help me to learn to wait patiently for You. Amen.

Peace Rules

And let the peace that comes from Christ rule in your hearts.
For as members of one body you are called to live in peace.

COLOSSIANS 3:15 NLT

Peace is a way of living our lives. It happens when we let Christ's peace into our lives to rule over our emotions, our doubts, and our worries, and then go one step more and let His peace control the way we live. Peace is God's gift of grace to us, but it is also the way to a graceful life, the path to harmony with the world around us.

Jesus, what an amazing gift of peace that comes from You.
Thank You for leading me on the path of a graceful life. Amen.

The Center of Our Lives

The apostles often met together
and prayed with a single purpose in mind.
ACTS 1:14 CEV

What do you do when you get together with the people you're close to? You probably talk and laugh, share a meal, maybe go shopping or work on a project. But do you ever pray together? If prayer is the center of our lives, we will want to share this gift of grace with those with whom we're closest.

Heavenly Father, when I meet together regularly with
my sisters and brothers, nudge us to pray with a single
purpose, keeping You in the center and
uniting us with Your love. Amen.

See Jesus

God left nothing that is not subject to them. Yet at present
we do not see everything subject to them. But we do see Jesus.

HEBREWS 2:8–9 NIV

We know that Jesus has won the victory over sin, and yet
when we look at the world as it is right now, we still see sin all
around us. We see pain and suffering, greed and selfishness,
brokenness and despair. We know that the world is not ruled
by God. Yet despite that, we can look past the darkness of
sin. By grace, right now, we can see Jesus.

Jesus, when I am overwhelmed by the evil that seems to be
winning in this world, remind me that You have won
the victory. Give me the grace to see You. Amen.

Relax. . .

But I am calm and quiet, like a baby with its mother.
I am at peace, like a baby with its mother.

PSALM 131:2 NCV

You know how a baby lies completely limp in her mother's arms, totally trusting and at peace? That is the attitude you need to practice. Let yourself relax in God's arms, wrapped in His grace. Life will go on around you, with all its noise and turmoil. Meanwhile, you are completely safe, totally secure, without a worry in the world. Lie back and enjoy the quiet!

Heavenly Father, thank You for the peace You provide.
Thank You that I can rest so gently and comfortably
in Your loving arms. Amen.

All Equal By Grace

Live in peace with each other. Do not be proud,
but make friends with those who seem unimportant.
Do not think how smart you are.

ROMANS 12:16 NCV

Sometimes other people just seem so stupid! We pride ourselves that we would never act like that, dress like that, talk like that. But God wants us to let go of our pride. He wants us to remember that in His eyes we are all equal, all loved, all saved only by grace.

Lord, Your Word is clear—pride keeps me from living
at peace with others. Cleanse me from pride,
and help me to focus on loving instead of judging. Amen.

Move On

Anyone who belongs to Christ has become a new person.
The old life is gone; a new life has begun!

2 CORINTHIANS 5:17 NLT

You are a brand-new person in Jesus! Don't worry about what came before. Don't linger over your guilt and regret. Move on. Step out into the new, grace-filled life Christ has given you.

Heavenly Father, how grateful I am for new life!
Thank You for putting to death the old me
and for giving me the promise of
a new life in Christ. Amen.

Quiet, Gentle Grace

*"Let me teach you, because I am humble and gentle at heart,
and you will find rest for your souls."*

MATTHEW 11:29 NLT

Sometimes we keep trying to do things on our own, even though we don't know what we're doing and even though we're exhausted. And all the while, Jesus waits quietly, ready to show us the way. He will lead us with quiet, gentle grace, carrying our burdens for us. We don't have to try so hard. We can finally rest.

Jesus, I don't like feeling incompetent and inadequate. It makes me feel anxious and exhausted. Thank You for Your gentle teaching and for the strength You provide. Give me Your rest. Amen.

Always Present

Lord, you have been watching. Do not keep quiet.
Lord, do not leave me alone.

PSALM 35:22 NCV

Have you ever seen a child suddenly look up from playing, realize she's all alone, and then run to get her mother's attention? Meanwhile, her mother was watching her all along. Sometimes solitude is a good thing—and other times, it's just plain lonely. When loneliness turns into isolation, remember that God's loving eyes are always on you. He will never leave you all alone, and His grace is always present.

Lord, how wonderful to know that You are always with me,
watching over me with tender, loving eyes. Help me to listen
to Your voice, remembering I am never alone. Amen.

Strong in Christ

I can do all things through Christ who strengthens me.
PHILIPPIANS 4:13 NKJV

Left to ourselves, we are weak. We make mistakes. We fall short of our goals. But in Christ, we are strong. By His grace, we can accomplish anything.

Jesus, I am conditioned to believe that weakness is something to be despised. Help me to see weakness differently—remembering that my weakness is a conduit for Your strength. Amen.

Careful Plans

Without good advice everything goes wrong—
it takes careful planning for things to go right.

PROVERBS 15:22 CEV

The Bible reminds us that when we start a new venture, we should not trust success to come automatically. We need to seek out the advice of those we trust. We need to make careful plans. And most of all, we need to seek God's counsel, praying for the grace and wisdom to do things right.

Father, there are so many opportunities for me to grab hold
of. It's tempting to dive in headfirst. I desperately need Your
counsel. Fill me with Your grace and wisdom. Amen.

From God

There are different kinds of gifts,
but they are all from the same Spirit.

1 Corinthians 12:4 ncv

God shines through us in different ways. One person is good at expressing herself in words, another is good with children, and still another has a gift for giving wise counsel to her friends. Whatever our gifts are, they all come from God. They are all tangible expressions of His grace.

Heavenly Father, Giver of all good gifts, I am amazed
at Your creativity and Your Spirit shining through each of
Your children. Help me to use my gifts for Your glory. Amen.

Meant to Move

*We are only foreigners living here on earth for a while,
just as our ancestors were. And we will soon be gone,
like a shadow that suddenly disappears.*

1 Chronicles 29:15 CEV

We are not meant to feel too at home in this world. Maybe that is why time is designed to keep us from lingering too long in one place. We are meant to be moving on, making our way to our forever-home in heaven. Grace has brought us safe thus far—and grace will lead us home.

*Father, the old song says, "This world is not my home,
I'm just passing through. . ." How I long for the treasure of
my heavenly home. I cannot wait to be there with You. Amen.*

What's Real

---

*"Then you will experience for yourselves the truth,
and the truth will free you."*

JOHN 8:32 MSG

Truth is what is real, while lies are nothing but words. God wants us to experience what is truly real. Sometimes we would rather hide from reality, but grace comes to us through truth. No matter how painful the truth may sometimes seem, it will ultimately set us free.

---

*Jesus, thank You for the truth that sets me free.
Help me to discern truth from lies. Allow me to
experience Your truth in the depths of my being. Amen.*

Growing in Grace

This is my prayer for you: that your love will grow more and more; that you will have knowledge and understanding with your love.

PHILIPPIANS 1:9 NCV

God wants us to be spiritually mature. He wants us to love more deeply, and at the same time, He wants us to reach deeper into wisdom and understanding. This is not something we can accomplish in our own strength with our own abilities. Only God can make us grow in grace.

God, I long for my love to grow more and more.
Fill me with knowledge and understanding;
help me to lean into Your grace that brings growth. Amen.

Grace Multiplied

Honor the LORD with your wealth
and with the best part of everything you produce.

PROVERBS 3:9 NLT

Wе connect the word *wealth* with money, but long ago the word meant "happiness, prosperity, well-being." If you think about your wealth in this light, then the word encompasses far more of your life. Your health, your abilities, your friends, your family, your physical strength, and your creative energy—all of these are parts of your true wealth. Grace brought all of these riches into your life, and when we use them to honor God, grace is multiplied still more.

Father, when I consider all the good things You have given
me, I am rich beyond belief. Help me to graciously
honor You with my wealth. Amen.

Building God's Kingdom

I have filled him with the Spirit of God, in wisdom and skill,
in understanding and intelligence, in knowledge,
and in all kinds of craftsmanship.

EXODUS 31:3 AMP

Your abilities, your intelligence, your knowledge, and your talents are all gifts of grace from God's generous Spirit. But without wisdom, the ability to see into the spiritual world, none of these gifts is worth very much. Wisdom is what fits together all of the other pieces, allowing us to use our talents to build God's spiritual kingdom.

Lord, I am so grateful for the filling of Your Spirit and for
the gift of wisdom. Thank You for allowing me to be
involved with the building of Your kingdom. Amen.

Heaven's Perspective

*Always give yourselves fully to the work of the Lord,
because you know that your labor in the Lord is not in vain.*

1 CORINTHIANS 15:58 NIV

You may feel sometimes as though all of your hard work comes to nothing. But if your work is the Lord's work, you can trust Him to bring it to fulfillment. You may not always know what is being accomplished in the light of eternity, but God knows. And when you look back from heaven's perspective, you will be able to see how much grace was accomplished through all of your hard work.

*God, when I don't see results, I sometimes get discouraged
in my work for You. Help me to remember that You
are busy doing things I cannot see. Amen.*

A Solid Foundation

A bad motive can't achieve a good end.

PROVERBS 17:20 MSG

We hear it all the time: The end justifies the means. But that is not how it works in the kingdom of God. It's like trying to build a beautiful house on a shaky foundation. It just doesn't work. Sooner or later, the weak foundation will affect the rest of the house. True achievement is built on God's grace and love. That is the kind of foundation that holds solid no matter what.

Father, fill my heart with the longing and motivation to do Your work. Help me to build that work on the solid foundation of Your grace and love. Amen.

Focus Point

Therefore. . .stand firm. Let nothing move you.
1 CORINTHIANS 15:58 NIV

Some days stress comes at us from all directions. Our emotions are overwhelming. Life makes us dizzy. On days like that, don't worry about getting a lot accomplished—and don't try to make enormous leaps in your spiritual life. Instead, simply stand in one place. Like a ballet dancer who looks at one point to keep her balance while she twirls, fix your eyes on Jesus.

Jesus, when I get caught up in the whirlwind of stress and busyness and my own agenda, I can easily lose my balance. Help me to fix my eyes on You. Amen.

Truths

*For the word of God is alive and powerful. It is sharper
than the sharpest two-edged sword, cutting between
soul and spirit, between joint and marrow.
It exposes our innermost thoughts and desires.*

HEBREWS 4:12 NLT

God's words are not merely letters on a page. They are
living things that work their way into our hearts and minds,
revealing the fears and hopes we've kept hidden away, sometimes even from ourselves. Like a doctor's scalpel that cuts
in order to heal, God's Word slices through our carefully
created facades and exposes our deepest truths.

*Father, how grateful I am for Your Word. I am amazed
at the way it teaches me and exposes my true intentions.
Help me to bravely submit myself to Your healing. Amen.*

Blessing Others

"Bless those who curse you.
Pray for those who hurt you."

LUKE 6:28 NLT

Not only does God bless us, but we are called to bless others. God wants to show the world His grace through us. He can do this when we show our commitment to make God's love real in the world around us through our words and actions, as well as through our prayer life. We offer blessings to others when we greet a scowl with a smile, when we refuse to respond to angry words, and when we offer understanding to those who are angry and hurt.

God, I sometimes forget that the world is watching.
I long to shine Your light to everyone I see. Help me to
bestow blessings on others, even when they hurt me. Amen.

Peace

"I will teach all your children,
and they will enjoy great peace."

ISAIAH 54:13 NLT

It's hard not to worry about the children in our lives. Many dangers threaten them, and our world is so uncertain. We can do our best to teach and guide the children we love, but in the end we must trust them to God's grace, knowing that they must find their own relationship with Him—and that as they know Him, they will find peace, even in the midst of the world's uncertainty.

Heavenly Father, thank You for the children in my life.
Help me to remember that You love them even more than
I do and that You hold them in Your loving arms. Amen.

Sound Advice

Without good direction, people lose their way;
the more wise counsel you follow, the better your chances.

PROVERBS 11:14 MSG

Often God makes use of other people when He wants to guide you. His grace flows to you through others' experiences and wisdom. Keep your ears open for His voice speaking to you through the good advice of those you trust.

Lord, even when I am inclined to run off on my own,
help me to seek direction from the wise people in my life. Amen.

Christlike

Don't sin by letting anger control you.
Think about it overnight and remain silent.

PSALM 4:4 NLT

A disciple must practice certain skills until she becomes good at them. As Christ's disciples, we are called to live like Him. The challenge of that calling is often hardest in life's small, daily frustrations, especially with the people we love the most. But as we practice saying no to anger, controlling it rather than allowing it to control us, God's grace helps us develop new skills, even ones we never thought possible!

God, teach me the difference between sinful anger
and righteous anger. Help me to push the "pause"
button when I get angry so I can listen to You. Amen.

Reach Out to Others

*Whoever has the gift of encouraging
others should encourage.*

ROMANS 12:8 NCV

Just as God encourages us, He wants us to encourage others. The word *encourage* comes from Latin words that mean "to put heart or inner strength into someone." When God encourages us, His own heart reaches out to us and His strength becomes ours. As we rely on His grace, we are empowered to turn and reach out to those around us, lending them our hearts and strength.

*Lord, thank You for reaching out to me with Your heart
and giving me Your strength. I pray that I would
use that strength to encourage others. Amen.*

Unfailing Love

But I trust in your unfailing love.
I will rejoice because you have rescued me.

Psalm 13:5 nlt

Have you ever done that exercise in trust where you fall backward into another person's arms? It's hard to let yourself drop, trusting that the other person will catch you. The decision to let yourself fall is not an emotion that sweeps over you. It's just something you have to do, despite your fear. In the same way, we commit ourselves to God's unfailing love, finding new joy each time His arms keep us from falling.

Father, You have shown me time and time again that I can trust You because You have consistently rescued me with Your unfailing love. I commit myself to Your loving arms. Amen.

Family Ties

Jesus, who makes people holy, and those who are made
holy are from the same family. So he is not ashamed
to call them his brothers and sisters.

HEBREWS 2:11 NCV

You and Jesus are family! Jesus, the One who made you
whole and clean in God's sight, is your Brother. Family
ties connect you to Him and to all those with whom He is
connected. In Christ, we find new connections with each
other. By His grace, we are now kinfolk.

Jesus, my Brother, how grateful I am to be a part of Your
holy family. Thank You for making me whole and
clean and for inviting me into Your fold. Amen.

Back to God

My dear brothers and sisters, always be willing to listen and slow to speak. Do not become angry easily, because anger will not help you live the right kind of life God wants.

JAMES 1:19–20 NCV

Our feelings are gifts from God, and we should never be ashamed of them. Instead, we need to offer them all back to God, both our joys and our frustrations. When we give God our anger, our irritation, our hurt feelings, and our frustrations, we make room in our hearts to truly hear what others are saying.

Father, as uncomfortable as my feelings can be sometimes, thank You for what they teach me. Help me to trust You with all my feelings so I can be a good listener. Amen.

Healthy

"Give us today our daily bread."

MATTHEW 6:11 NIV

We need food each day. Healthy fruits and vegetables, whole grains, lean protein for our bodies—and times of prayer and quiet for our souls. Like a loving mother, God delights in nourishing His children.

Father, You provide everything I need. Help me to make wise choices—to fill myself with healthy foods and the nourishment of Your presence. Amen.

Wholly and Completely

"Forgive others, and you will be forgiven."
LUKE 6:37 NLT

The words *forgive* and *pardon* come from very old words that mean "to give up completely and wholeheartedly." When we forgive others, we totally give up our rights to feel we've been injured or slighted. And in return, God's grace totally fills the gaps left behind when we let go of our own selfishness. As we give ourselves wholeheartedly to others, God gives Himself completely to us.

God, help me to forgive others so that nothing hinders me
from fully receiving the gift of Your forgiveness.
Thank You for Your grace that pours over me. Amen.

Our Companion

Our LORD, you are the friend of your worshipers,
and you make an agreement with all of us.

PSALM 25:14 CEV

God is our Friend. He is our companion through life's journey; He is the One who always understands us; and no matter what we do, He always accepts us and loves us. What better agreement could we ever have with anyone than what we have with God?

Father, thank You for being my Friend, my companion,
my comfort. Thank You for the everlasting covenant You
have made with me. I am grateful to be Your child. Amen.

The Next Oasis

*The LORD will always guide you and provide good things
to eat when you are in the desert. He will make you healthy.
You will be like a garden that has plenty of water
or like a stream that never runs dry.*

ISAIAH 58:11 CEV

God wants you to be healthy—not just physically, but emotionally, intellectually, and spiritually as well. He wants to fill your life full of all the things you truly need. The life He wants for you is not dry and empty and barren. Instead, it is lush and full of delicious things to nourish you. We all have to cross life's deserts sometimes, but even then God will supply what you need to reach the next oasis He has waiting.

*Lord, this life can feel like an incredibly long journey,
especially when I am in the desert. Sustain and strengthen
me with the promises of Your Word. Amen.*

Wonderful Things

Everything God made is waiting with excitement for
God to show his children's glory completely.

ROMANS 8:19 NCV

Some days it's hard to feel very optimistic. We listen to the evening news and hear story after story about natural disasters and human greed. God doesn't want us to be ostriches, hiding our heads in the sand, refusing to acknowledge what's going on in the world. But He also wants us to believe that the future is full of wonderful things He has planned. The whole world is holding its breath, waiting for God's wonderful grace to reveal itself.

God, I cannot even begin to comprehend the riches You have
in store for us, Your children. When I am discouraged,
lift my head and remind me of Your promise. Amen.

Good for You!

A happy heart is like good medicine,
but a broken spirit drains your strength.

PROVERBS 17:22 NCV

God longs to make you happy. He knows that happiness is good for you. Mentally and physically, you function better when you are happy. Discouragement and sadness sap your strength. It's like trying to work while carrying a heavy load on your back: It slows you down and makes everything harder. Let God heal the breaks in your spirit. His grace can make you strong and happy.

Father, I know the heaviness of a broken spirit.
Heal me and help me carry my burdens. Remind me of
the reasons I have to be grateful and happy. Amen.

The Entire Package

He makes the whole body fit together perfectly. As each part
does its own special work, it helps the other parts grow,
so that the whole body is healthy and growing and full of love.

EPHESIANS 4:16 NLT

God has a holistic perspective on health. He sees your body,
soul, heart, and mind, and He wants each part of you to be
strong and fit. He looks at our world in the same way, longing
to heal the entire package—society, the environment, and
governments. He wants His body on earth, the Church, to be
whole and strong as well. Health pours out of Him, a daily
stream of grace on which we can rely for each aspect of life.

Lord, I am grateful You have enabled me to be a part
of Your Body—the Church. Help me to do my
part so that all of us can grow. Amen.

Breathing

*In certain ways we are weak, but the Spirit is here to help us.
For example, when we don't know what to pray for, the Spirit
prays for us in ways that cannot be put into words.*

ROMANS 8:26 CEV

The Holy Spirit is the wind that blows through our world,
breathing grace and life into everything that exists. He will
breathe through you as well as you open yourself to Him.
We need not worry about our own weakness or mistakes,
for the Spirit will make up for them. His creative power
will pray through us, work through us, and love through us.

*Holy Spirit, thank You for interceding on my behalf,
for breathing grace and life into me. Even through
my weakness, thank You for Your power that
carries my very breath to God. Amen.*

A Special Place

*My people will live in peaceful places
and in safe homes and in calm places of rest.*

ISAIAH 32:18 NCV

Home is the place where you feel most comfortable—the place where you can kick off your shoes, put on your bathrobe, and relax. God has created this place for you, a place where His grace can soothe your heart in a special way.

God, despite the chaos in this world, thank You for providing me with places of sanctuary. I invite You in—please make my heart Your home and give me rest. Amen.

An Attitude

God proves to be good to the man who passionately waits,
to the woman who diligently seeks. It's a good thing
to quietly hope, quietly hope for help from God.

LAMENTATIONS 3:25 MSG

Hope is an attitude, not an emotion. It means putting our whole hearts into relying on God. It means keeping our eyes focused on Him no matter what, waiting for Him to reveal Himself in our lives. God never disappoints those who passionately wait for His help, who diligently seek His grace.

God, help me to passionately wait and diligently seek.
Help me not to be frantic, but to quietly hope for
the help that is sure to come from You. Amen.

Grace in Return

"Then those 'sheep' are going to say, 'Master, what are you talking
about? When did we ever see you hungry and feed you, thirsty
and give you a drink?...' Then the King will say, 'I'm telling the
solemn truth: Whenever you did one of these things to someone
overlooked or ignored, that was me—you did it to me.'"

MATTHEW 25:37–40 MSG

If Christ were sitting on our doorstep, lonely and tired and
hungry, what would we do? We like to think we would throw the
door wide open and welcome Him into our home. But the truth is
we're given the opportunity to offer our hospitality to Jesus each
time we're faced with a person in need. His grace reaches out to
us through those who feel misunderstood and overlooked, and
He wants us to offer that same grace back in return.

*Jesus, open my eyes to the hungry and thirsty people all
around me. Whether their hunger is spiritual or physical or
both, help me to give them Your grace. Amen.*

All of You

> " 'Love the Lord God with all your passion
> and prayer and intelligence and energy.' "
>
> MARK 12:30 MSG

God wants all of you. He wants the "spiritual parts," but He also wants your emotions, your physical energy, and your brain's intelligence. Offer them all to God as expressions of your love for Him. Let His grace use every part of you!

God, I sometimes forget that You want all of me.
I dedicate my emotions, my energy, and my intelligence to You.
Enable me to offer these as expressions of Your love. Amen.

Harmony

*The hope of the righteous [those of honorable character and
integrity] is joy, but the expectation of the wicked [those who
oppose God and ignore His wisdom] comes to nothing.*

PROVERBS 10:28 AMP

When we try to live our lives apart from God, we put
ourselves in a place where we can no longer see His grace.
Joy comes from being in harmony with God.

*Father, when I try to live apart from You, gently pull me
back into Your arms. Shower me with grace and
the joy of living in harmony with You. Amen.*

Freely Given

*Out of sheer generosity he put us in right standing with
himself. A pure gift. He got us out of the mess we're in
and restored us to where he always wanted us to be.
And he did it by means of Jesus Christ.*

ROMANS 3:24 MSG

How kind God has been to us! He brought us close to
Himself. He reached down and picked us up out of our messy
lives. He healed us so we could be the people we were always
meant to be. That is what grace is: a gift we never deserved,
freely given out of love.

*Oh kind, gracious, and generous heavenly Father, thank You
for the gift of Your Son, for pulling me out of the mess and
restoring me to a right relationship with You. Amen.*

Trust Him

You people who are now crying are blessed,
because you will laugh with joy.

Luke 6:21 NCV

God's grace comes to you even in the midst of tears. He is there with you in your hurt and your sadness. Trust in Him, knowing that sadness does not last forever. One day you will laugh again.

Father, even in my darkest days, bestow on me Your grace.
Thank You for the promise that my tears will not last
and that You will replace them with joy. Amen.

Surrender

"For whoever wants to save their life will lose it,
but whoever loses their life for me will save it."

LUKE 9:24 NIV

Life is full of paradoxes. God seems to delight in turning our ideas inside out and backward. It doesn't seem to make sense, but the only way to possess our life is to surrender it absolutely into God's hands. As we let go of everything, God's grace gives everything back to us, transformed by His love.

God, even when Your Word doesn't completely make sense,
help me to trust You implicitly. Give me the strength to
surrender every part of my life to You. Amen.

Act in Love

Let all that you do be done in love.

1 Corinthians 16:14 NRSV

Because love is not merely an emotion, it needs to become real through action. We grow in love as we act in love. Some days the emotion may overwhelm us; other days we may feel nothing at all. But if we express our love while making meals, driving the car, talking to our families, or cleaning the house, God's love will flow through us to the world around us—and we will see His grace at work.

Father, when I feel love, it's easy to show it. But the feelings are not always there. Help me to find ways to obediently express Your love through all my actions. Amen.

What You Need

Give me neither poverty nor riches!
Give me just enough to satisfy my needs.

PROVERBS 30:8 NLT

God gives us what we need, and He knows exactly what and how much that is. Whatever He has given you financially, He knows that is what you need right now. Trust His grace. He will satisfy your needs.

Father, my Provider, I thank You for giving me exactly what I need. Help me to trust You with Your provision for me and to know that Your grace is always enough for me. Amen.

Christ Followers

"This is what the LORD All-Powerful says: 'Do what is right and true. Be kind and merciful to each other.'"

ZECHARIAH 7:9 NCV

As Christ's followers, we need to interact with others the way He did when He was on earth. That means we don't lie to each other, and we don't use others. Instead, we practice kindness and mercy. We let God's grace speak through our mouths.

Lord all-powerful, thank You for the blessing of relationships. Help me to do what is right and true, to be kind and merciful to others. Give me Your grace always. Speak through me. Amen.

Renewal

"Look, the winter is past, and the rains are over and gone."

SONG OF SOLOMON 2:11 NLT

Dreary times of cold and rain come to us all. Just as the earth needs those times to renew itself, so do we. As painful as those times are, grace works through them to make us into the people God has called us to be. But once those times are over, there's no need to continue to dwell on them. Go outside and enjoy the sunshine!

Father, it's easy to become discouraged during the long days of winter. But I know times of darkness are necessary to fully appreciate the joy of light. Help me to revel in Your sunlight. Amen.

Quiet Grace

Patient persistence pierces through indifference;
gentle speech breaks down rigid defenses.

PROVERBS 25:15 MSG

When we're in the midst of an argument, we often become fixated on winning. We turn conflicts into power struggles, and we want to come out the victor. By sheer force, if necessary, we want to shape people to our will. But that is not the way God treats us. His grace is gentle and patient rather than loud and forceful. We need to follow His example and let His quiet grace speak through us in His timing rather than ours.

Father, thank You for the gentleness of Your grace. Give me a
spirit of patient persistence. Instill my words with gentleness.
May I always value relationships over being right. Amen.

Alone Time with God

But Jesus often withdrew to the wilderness for prayer.
LUKE 5:16 NLT

God is always with us, even when we're too busy to do more than whisper a prayer in the shower or as we drive the car. But if even Jesus needed to make time to get away by Himself for some alone time with God, then we certainly need to do so, too. In those quiet moments of prayer, by ourselves with God, we will find the grace we need to live our busy lives.

Jesus, thank You for Your constant presence with me.
Help me to make time with You a priority,
knowing that putting You first will make
everything else fall into place. Amen.

Constant Grace

*For Jesus doesn't change—yesterday, today,
tomorrow, he's always totally himself.*

HEBREWS 13:8 MSG

As human beings, we live in the stream of time. Sometimes all the changes time brings terrify us; sometimes they fill us with joy and excitement. Either way, we can cling to the still point that lies in the middle of our changing world: Jesus Christ, who never changes. His constant grace leads us through all life's changes, and one day it will bring us to our home in heaven, beyond time, where we will be like Him.

Jesus, how grateful I am that You stay the same. Yesterday, today, and forever, I can count on You to remain firm and steadfast, no matter how much change life brings. Amen.

New Strength

"In quietness and confidence is your strength."

ISAIAH 30:15 NLT

The weaker we feel, the more we fret. The more we fret, the weaker we feel. It's a vicious circle. Stop the circle! Find a quiet place, if only for a few moments, to draw close to God. Grace will come to you through the quiet, and you will discover new strength.

Father, I desperately need You. Step in and take me out of the vicious circle of worry and fretting. Give me Your peace. Thank You for Your strength. Amen.

Only by Grace

*Accept one another, then, just as Christ accepted you,
in order to bring praise to God.*

ROMANS 15:7 NIV

It's easy to pick out others' faults. Sometimes you may even feel justified in doing so, as though God will approve of your righteousness as you point out others' sinfulness. Don't forget that Christ accepted you, with all your brokenness and faults. Only by grace were you made whole. Share that grace—that acceptance and unconditional love—with the people around you.

*Jesus, what a joy it is to know that You have accepted me
just as I am! You have made me whole. Help me to
pass that grace on to others. Amen.*

Fresh Hearts

"I will give you a new heart and put a new spirit within you."
ЕZEKIEL 36:26 NKJV

Life is full of irritations and hassles. Bills to pay, errands to run, arguments to settle, and endless responsibilities all stress our hearts until we feel old and worn. But God renews us. Day after day, over and over, His grace comes to us, making our hearts fresh and green and growing.

Lord, when I focus on earthly things, my heart is small. Expand my heart and give me a heavenly perspective, knowing that You will redeem and make all things new. Amen.

Sleep in Peace

*At day's end I'm ready for sound sleep, for you,
GOD, have put my life back together.*

PSALM 4:8 MSG

At the end of the day, let everything—good and bad together—drop into God's hands. You can sleep in peace, knowing that meanwhile God will continue to work, healing all that is broken in your life. Relax in His grace.

Father, thank You for the gift of rest—a time to put the busyness aside. When I wake, things make much more sense. Thank You for putting my life back together! Amen.

All Alone

"But when you pray, go away by yourself, shut the door behind you, and pray to your Father in private. Then your Father, who sees everything, will reward you."

MATTHEW 6:6 NLT

Prayer takes many shapes and forms. There's the corporate kind of prayer, in which we open our hearts to God as part of a congregation. There is also the kind of prayer that is said quickly and on the run. But we need to make at least some time in our lives for prayer in the privacy of some quiet place, when we meet God's grace all alone.

Lord, how I need You. Every moment of every day, I need Your presence. Gently lead me into Your loving arms, to set aside precious, quiet time with You. Amen.

Today and Tomorrow

You are my strong shield, and I trust you completely.
You have helped me, and I will celebrate
and thank you in song.

PSALM 28:7 CEV

God proves Himself to us over and over again. And yet over and over, we doubt His power. We need to learn from experience. The God whose strength rescued us yesterday and the day before will certainly rescue us again today. As we celebrate the grace we received yesterday and the day before, we gain confidence and faith for today and tomorrow.

My Father, my Strong Shield, You have proved yourself
to me over and over again. Remind me of Your goodness.
I praise You and celebrate Your faithfulness. Amen.

Wonderful!

Commit your actions to the LORD,
and your plans will succeed.

PROVERBS 16:3 NLT

Just because we want something to happen, doesn't mean it will, no matter how hard we pray. We've all found that out (often to our sorrow!). But when we truly commit everything we do to God, praying only for His grace to be given free rein in our lives, then we will be surprised by what comes about. It may not be what we imagined—but it will be wonderful!

Father, Your Word tells me that Your ways are not my
ways. I pray that I would graciously commit all my
plans to You, armed with the promise that
You will help them succeed. Amen.

Use Your Gift

---

*Each of you has been blessed with one of God's
many wonderful gifts to be used in the
service of others. So use your gift well.*

1 PETER 4:10 CEV

God did not give you your talents for your own pleasure
only. These skills you have were meant to be offered to
the world. He wants to use them to build His kingdom
here on earth. So pick up your skill, whatever it is, and
use it to bring grace to someone's life.

---

*Lord, thank You for the blessing of Your wonderful gifts.
Help me to identify the gifts You have given me, and help me
to use them well to bless others and honor You. Amen.*

Young

Honor and enjoy your Creator while you're still young.

ECCLESIASTES 12:1 MSG

Young is a matter of perspective. Some people are old at fifteen, and others are still young at ninety. As we enjoy the God who made us, honoring Him in all we do, His grace will keep us young.

Father, my Creator, instill within my spirit a longing to honor You and enjoy You all the days of my life. May Your grace continue to amaze me and keep me young. Amen.

On Truth's Side

We're rooting for the truth to win out in you.
We couldn't possibly do otherwise.

2 Corinthians 13:8 msg

As we look at the world around us, we can see that people often prefer falsehoods to truth. They choose to live in a world that soothes their anxiety, rather than face life's reality. We cannot force people to acknowledge what they don't want to face, but we can do all we can to encourage them and build them up. We can cheer for the truth, trusting that God's grace is always on truth's side.

Father, Author of Truth, open my eyes to the truth
of Your Word. Help me not to be swayed by
falsehood, but instead to cling to Your truth. Amen.

Most Important

Tune your ears to the world of Wisdom;
set your heart on a life of Understanding.

PROVERBS 2:3 MSG

What do you listen to most? Do you hear the world's voice, telling you to buy, buy, buy; to dress and look a certain way; to focus on things that won't last? Or have you tuned your ears to hear the quiet voice of God's wisdom? You can tell the answer to that question by your response to yet another question: What is most important to you? Things? Or the intangible grace of true understanding?

Lord, You are Wisdom. Tune my heart to Your wise voice.
Make Your priorities my priorities, and fill my heart with
Your wisdom and Your understanding. Amen.

Never Bought

They trust in their riches and brag about all of their wealth.
You cannot buy back your life or pay off God!
PSALM 49:6–7 CEV

We humans are easily confused about what real wealth is. We think that money can make us strong. We assume that physical possessions will enhance our importance and dignity in others' eyes. But life is not for sale. And grace can never be bought.

Heavenly Father, I am tempted to trust in worldly riches,
but I know they will never truly satisfy. Help me to long
for true wealth, which lies in the promise
of eternal life with You. Amen.

Nothing More Valuable

Wisdom is more valuable than gold and crystal.
It cannot be purchased with jewels mounted in fine gold.

JOB 28:17 NLT

Money can't buy you love—and it can't buy wisdom either. Wisdom is more precious than anything this world has to offer. In fact, some passages of the Old Testament seem to indicate that Wisdom is another name for Jesus. Just as Jesus is the Way, the Truth, and the Life, He is also the One who gives us the vision to see God's world all around us. No other gift is more valuable than Jesus.

Jesus, the Way, the Truth, and the Life, give me Your vision.
Help me to see the world through Your eyes. Help me to
place my relationship with You above all else. Amen.

The Bigger Picture

"But you, be strong and do not lose courage,
for there is reward for your work."

2 CHRONICLES 15:7 NASB

Why do you work? For a paycheck? For respect? For a sense of self-worth? All of those things are good reasons to work, but never forget that your work is part of a bigger picture. God wants to use your hands, your intelligence, and your efforts to build His kingdom, the place where grace dwells.

*Father, help me to be strong, fill me with courage,
and give me confidence in knowing that You will
reward my work. I commit all I do to You. Amen.*

Perfection

I don't mean to say that I have already achieved these things or that I have already reached perfection. But I press on to possess that perfection for which Christ Jesus first possessed me.

PHILIPPIANS 3:12 NLT

We are called to be perfect. Nothing else is good enough for God's people. That doesn't mean we have an inflated sense of our own worth. And it doesn't mean we beat ourselves up when we fall short of perfection. We know that in our own strength we can never hope to achieve perfection—but with God's grace, anything is possible.

Jesus, when I am weary, give me the strength to keep pressing forward toward perfection. I want, more than anything, to be like You. Fill me with Your grace. Amen.

Grounded in Love

*"You'll be built solid, grounded in righteousness,
far from any trouble—nothing to fear!"*

Isaiah 54:12 MSG

Balance isn't something we can achieve in ourselves. Just when we think we have it all together, life has a tendency to come crashing down around our ears. But even in the midst of life's most chaotic moments, God gives us grace; He keeps us balanced in His love. Like a building that is built to sway in an earthquake without falling down, we will stay standing if we remain grounded in His love.

*Heavenly Father, keep me grounded in Your love.
Provide for me a strong foundation to keep me
stable through life's most chaotic moments.
Thank You for Your steady hand. Amen.*

For Generations

*I inherited your book on living; it's mine forever—
what a gift! And how happy it makes me!*

PSALM 119:111 MSG

Think of it! God's Word is ours. We can hear His voice in scripture—and apply it to our own lives. Generation upon generation has followed this amazing book of life, and now it is our turn. In the Bible, each and every day, we find God's grace revealed.

Father, Your Word is such a gift. Thank You for sharing Your heart with me through scripture and for its endurance through all generations. Help me to treasure Your Word. Amen.

Walk Confidently

*"But blessed are those who trust in the L*ORD
*and have made the L*ORD *their hope and confidence."*
JEREMIAH 17:7 NLT

W hat gives you confidence? Is it your clothes. . .your money. . .your skills? These are all good things, but they are blessings from God, given to you through His grace. When your hopes (in other words, your expectations for the future) rest only in God, then you can walk confidently, knowing He will never disappoint you.

Lord, You are my hope and my confidence. I place all my
expectations for the future in You, knowing that You will
never disappoint me. Thank You for Your love. Amen.

A Special Kind of Grace

*Oh, how blessed are you parents, with your quivers full of
children! Your enemies don't stand a chance against you;
you'll sweep them right off your doorstep.*

PSALM 127:4–5 MSG

What are your worst enemies? Despair? Self-doubt? Selfishness? We all face enemies like these. But God's grace comes to us in a special way through children. As we love them, we find hope; we focus outward and forget about ourselves. And somehow those funny little people manage to sweep our enemies right off the doorsteps of our hearts!

*Heavenly Father, thank You for the blessing of little children.
Thank You for the way they bring hope and simplicity
to my life, putting even my darkest circumstances
in perspective. Amen.*

Grace for Each Day

*May the Lord direct your hearts into God's love
and Christ's perseverance.*

2 THESSALONIANS 3:5 NIV

Allow God to lead you each day. His grace will lead you
deeper and deeper into the love of God—a love that heals
your wounds and works through you to touch those around
you. Just as Christ never gave up but let love lead Him all
the way to the cross, so, too, God will direct you all the
way, giving you the strength and the courage you need to
face each challenge.

*Lord, direct my heart into Your love and into
the perseverance of Christ. Lead me, by Your grace,
into a deeper love for You. Amen.*

Life's Circumstances

*My child, do not reject the LORD's discipline, and don't get
angry when he corrects you. The LORD corrects those he
loves, just as parents correct the child they delight in.*

PROVERBS 3:11–12 NCV

God doesn't send us to time-out, and He certainly doesn't
take us over His knee and spank us. Instead, His discipline
comes to us through the circumstances of life. By saying yes
to whatever we face, no matter how difficult and frustrating
it may be, we allow God's grace to infuse each moment of
our day. We may be surprised to find that even in life's most
discouraging moments, God's love was waiting all along.

*Father, it can be difficult to accept Your discipline.
Help me to recognize when You are correcting me
and to see it as an outpouring of Your love
and Your delight. Amen.*

Reciprocal

When we get together, I want to encourage you in your faith,
but I also want to be encouraged by yours.

ROMANS 1:12 NLT

Encouragement is always reciprocal. When we encourage others, we are ourselves encouraged. In the world's economy, we pay a price in order to receive something we want; in other words, we give up something to get something. But in God's economy, we always get back what we give up. We are connected to each other, like parts of a body. Whatever good things we do for another are good for us as well.

God, thank You for the encouragement I find from
my brothers and sisters in You. Help me to both share
and receive the encouragement of Your love. Amen.

Safe in Christ

This is what God commands: that we believe in his Son,
Jesus Christ, and that we love each other,
just as he commanded.

1 JOHN 3:23 NCV

Again and again, the Bible links faith and love. Our human tendency is to put up walls of selfishness around ourselves, to protect ourselves at all costs. God asks us instead to believe daily that we are safe in Christ and to allow ourselves to be vulnerable as we reach out in love to those around us.

Father God, Your commands are not burdensome.
You ask me to believe in Your Son and to love others.
Give me the grace to obey You with all my heart. Amen.

No Division

*In Christ's family there can be no division into Jew
and non-Jew, slave and free, male and female.
Among us you are all equal.*

Galatians 3:28 msg

Grace is a gift that none of us deserve—and by grace Jesus has removed all barriers between God and ourselves. God asks that as members of His family we also knock down all the walls we've built between ourselves and others. Not just the obvious ones, but also the ones that may hide in our blind spots. In Christ, there is no liberal or conservative, no educated or uneducated, no division whatsoever.

*God, Your Son broke down all the walls. I am so grateful
that there is no longer any division among Your children.
Thank You for making us all equal in Your sight. Amen.*

Letting Go

A peaceful heart leads to a healthy body;
jealousy is like cancer in the bones.

PROVERBS 14:30 NLT

Some emotions are meant to be nourished, and others need to be quickly dropped into God's hands. Learn to cultivate and seek out that which brings peace to your heart. And practice letting go of your negative feelings as quickly as you can, releasing them to God. If you cling to these dark feelings, they will reproduce like a cancer, blocking the healthy flow of grace into your life.

Oh God, search me and know my heart. Expose any
negative feelings in me. Help me to leave them at the cross.
Cleanse me and fill my heart with Your peace. Amen.

Hungry

You serve me a six-course dinner right in front of my enemies.
You revive my drooping head; my cup brims with blessing.
PSALM 23:5 MSG

At the end of a long day, do you ever feel weak and ravenous with hunger? You've gone too long without eating, and now your body demands food! We often do the same thing to our spirits, depriving them of the spiritual nourishment they need—and then we wonder why life seems so overwhelming and bleak. But dinner is on the table, and God is waiting to revive us with platefuls of grace and cups brimming with blessings.

Father, I am so grateful that You know all of my needs
before I even ask. Thank You for reviving me and
for filling my cup with overflowing blessings. Amen.

Reasonable?

*"If you see your friend going wrong, correct him. If he responds,
forgive him. Even if it's personal against you and repeated
seven times through the day, and seven times he says,
'I'm sorry, I won't do it again,' forgive him."*

LUKE 17:3–4 MSG

As humans, we tend to feel that forgiveness has reasonable
limits. A person who repeats the same offense over and over
can't be very serious when he or she asks for forgiveness! It
makes sense from a human perspective. But fortunately for
us, God isn't reasonable. He forgives our sins no matter how
many times we repeat them. And He asks us to do the same
for others.

*Lord, I desperately need Your grace. Thank You for
offering me the gift of forgiveness, over and over again.
Help me to offer Your grace freely to others. Amen.*

Never Failing. . .

My friends scorn me, but I pour out my tears to God.

JOB 16:20 NLT

Sometimes even the best of friends can let you down. Human beings aren't perfect. But God's grace will never fail you. When even your closest friends don't understand you, take your hurt to Him.

*Lord, when I feel alone and rejected, I am so grateful
that I can pour out my tears to You. Thank You for
Your grace that never fails me. Amen.*

Expressions of Grace

*So I decided there is nothing better than to enjoy food and
drink and to find satisfaction in work. Then I realized
that these pleasures are from the hand of God.*

ECCLESIASTES 2:24 NLT

Hedonists are people who have decided that life's only
meaning lies in physical pleasures. But they can't escape
God's hand. Our food, our drink, the satisfaction we take
in our work, and all the physical pleasures of our lives
are not separate from God. Instead, they are expressions
of His grace. He longs for us to be fulfilled in every way
possible.

*Father, all good gifts come from You. You have bestowed
on me pleasures from Your hand. Help me to enjoy them
and use them to draw me closer to You. Amen.*

The Details

She is clothed with strength and dignity,
and she laughs without fear of the future.

PROVERBS 31:25 NLT

God wants to clothe us with His strength, His dignity. He wants us to be whole and competent, full of His grace. When we are, we can look at the future and laugh, knowing that God will take care of the details as we trust Him to be the foundation of our lives.

Father, thank You for clothing me with strength and dignity. Thank You that I can look to my future without fear, confident that You have all the details in Your hands. Amen.

Rescued!

The LORD wants to show his mercy to you. He wants to
rise and comfort you. The LORD is a fair God,
and everyone who waits for his help will be happy.

ISAIAH 30:18 NCV

God doesn't want you to feel lonely and unhappy. He waits
to bring you close to Him, to comfort you, to forgive you.
Wait for Him to rescue you from life's unhappiness. His grace
will never let you down. Keep your eyes fixed on Him, and
you will find happiness again.

Lord, how I long to receive Your mercy. Draw near to me,
rise up and comfort me, and give me happiness in
knowing Your help will rescue me. Amen.

Choosing Cheerful

A cheerful disposition is good for your health;
gloom and doom leave you bone-tired.
PROVERBS 17:22 MSG

Have you ever heard the saying "You may not be able to keep birds from perching on your head, but you can keep them from building nests in your hair"? It means we can't always control our emotions, but we can choose which ones we want to hold on to and dwell on. Choosing to be cheerful instead of gloomy is far healthier for our minds, bodies, and spirits. Being depressed is exhausting!

Father, when I am tempted to be gloomy and focus on
negative thoughts, turn my heart around. Help me to
focus on You, and fill my heart with cheer. Amen.

His Instrument

*"The Spirit of the Lord is on me, because he has anointed me
to proclaim good news to the poor. He has sent me to
proclaim freedom for the prisoners and recovery
of sight for the blind, to set the oppressed free."*

LUKE 4:18 NIV

Just as the Holy Spirit wants you to be free, He also wants
to use you as His instrument to breathe freedom and hope
into the world. Be His instrument today. Tell people the
truly good news that God loves them. Do whatever you can
to spread freedom and vision and hope. Be a vehicle of the
Spirit's grace.

*Lord, I long to be Your instrument. Give me the grace and
wisdom to spread Your message of good news and freedom
to the oppressed. Thank You for the hope You bring. Amen.*

Longing for Home

This is what the Lord says: "You will be in Babylon for seventy years. But then I will come and do for you all the good things I have promised, and I will bring you home again."

JEREMIAH 29:10 NLT

Sometimes in life we go through periods when we feel out of place, as though we just don't belong. Our hearts feel restless and lonely. We long to go home, but we don't know how. God uses those times to teach us special things we need to know. But He never leaves us in exile. His grace always brings us home.

Father, when I am in a season of loneliness and restlessness, help me to trust You to lead me home. Thank You for Your grace that guides me. Amen.

Everyone

If your enemy is hungry, feed him.
If he is thirsty, give him a drink.

PROVERBS 25:21 NCV

It's easy to have our friends over for dinner. Offering our hospitality to the people who give us pleasure is not much of a hardship. But hospitality gets harder when we offer it to the people who hurt our feelings, the people we really don't like very much. But God calls us to reach out in practical, tangible ways to everyone. Seek His grace to do this in some way every day.

Father, give me grace to love my enemies. Empower me to offer them the nourishment of Your love and the comfort of Your forgiveness, knowing that it leads me closer to You. Amen.

Brand-New Ways

Intelligent people are always ready to learn.
Their ears are open for knowledge.

PROVERBS 18:15 NLT

Whether you did well in school or not, you probably rely on your intelligence to get you through life. If you're really intelligent, though, you will remember that no matter how many years it has been since you graduated, you are never done learning. You need to be open to new ideas, willing to give up old, stale ways of thinking. When you are, you will find God's grace revealed in brand-new ways.

Father, thank You for the gift of knowledge.
Instill within me a heart that yearns to know more—
more of Your love and more of Your grace. Amen.

Eternal Joy

You make known to me the path of life;
you will fill me with joy in your presence,
with eternal pleasures at your right hand.

PSALM 16:11 NIV

God does not want you to be unhappy and confused. Believe in His grace. He is waiting to show you the way to go. He is longing to give you the joy of His presence. He wants to make you happy forever.

God, You have made Your ways known to me.
All I need to do is trust You and follow You,
and You will lead me to eternal pleasures. Amen.

Choose Grace

*And a servant of the Lord must not quarrel but
must be kind to everyone, a good teacher, and patient.*

2 TIMOTHY 2:24 NCV

Some days we can't help but feel irritated and out of sorts. But no matter how we feel on the inside, we can choose our outward behavior. We can make the decision to let disagreements go, to refuse to argue, to act in kindness, to show patience and a willingness to listen (even when we feel impatient). We can choose to walk in grace.

*Lord, help me to be kind to everyone, to be a good teacher,
and to be patient with others. Thank You for Your
grace that allows me to be Your servant. Amen.*

Witness of Laughter

We were filled with laughter, and we sang for joy.
And the other nations said, "What amazing things
the Lord has done for them."

PSALM 126:2 NLT

Life is truly amazing. Each day, grace touches us in many
ways, from the sun on our faces to each person we meet,
from the love of our friends and families to the satisfaction
of our work. Pay attention. Let people hear you laugh more.
Don't hide your joy. It's a witness to God's love.

Father, thank You for this amazing life and for Your grace
that touches me in so many ways. Help me to
wear my joy for all to see. Amen.

Radiant

---

*"If you are filled with light, with no dark corners,
then your whole life will be radiant, as though a
floodlight were filling you with light."*

LUKE 11:36 NLT

We all have dark corners in our lives we keep hidden.
We hide them from others. We hide them from God, and
we even try to hide them from ourselves. But God wants to
shine His light even into our darkest, most private nooks
and crannies. He wants us to step out into the floodlight of
His love—and then His grace will make us shine.

---

*Heavenly Father, fill me with light. Shine Your radiance on
all my dark corners. Remove my shame, and help me
to bask in the light of Your love. Amen.*

Amazing Love

Your unfailing love, O Lord, is as vast as the heavens;
your faithfulness reaches beyond the clouds.

PSALM 36:5 NLT

God loves you. The Creator of the Universe cares about you, and His love is unconditional and limitless. You can never make Him tired of you; He will never abandon you. You are utterly and completely loved, no matter what, forever and ever. Isn't that amazing?

Oh Father, I am so grateful for Your unfailing love,
vast as the heavens, reaching beyond the clouds.
Thank You for never abandoning me
and for Your amazing grace. Amen.

Depth of God's Riches

*Oh, the depth of the riches of the wisdom
and knowledge of God! How unsearchable his judgments,
and his paths beyond tracing out!*

ROMANS 11:33 NIV

Money is the way our culture measures value, but we forget that it's just a symbol, a unit of measurement that can never span the infinite value of God's grace. Imagine trying to use a tape measure to stretch across the galaxy or a teaspoon to determine how much water is in the sea. In the same way, money will always fall short if we use it to try to understand the depth of God's riches.

*Oh Father, there is no way I could begin to comprehend
Your greatness. Your wisdom and knowledge
would cause the oceans to overflow. Thank You for
sharing Your wealth with me. Amen.*

Overflowing Love

And may the Lord make your love for one another and for all people grow and overflow, just as our love for you overflows.

1 THESSALONIANS 3:12 NLT

As a very young child, you thought you were the center of the world. As you grew older, you had to go through the painful process of learning that others' feelings were as important as yours. God's grace wants to lift your perspective even higher, though. He wants you to overflow with love for other people.

Lord, fill my heart with love for others. As I learn to love You more and receive Your love, may my love for Your children overflow. Amen.

You Will Live

Their past sins will be forgiven, and they will live.
EZEKIEL 33:16 CEV

Do you ever feel doomed? Do you feel as though your mistakes are waiting to fall on your head, like a huge rock that will crush the life out of you? We all have moments like that. But God's grace doesn't let that enormous boulder drop. His forgiveness catches it and rolls it away. You will live after all!

Father, when I am discouraged and beaten down by the past, remind me of Your forgiveness and Your grace. Thank You for Your love that brings me life. Amen.

Another Moment Longer

Wait patiently for the Lord. Be brave and courageous.
Yes, wait patiently for the Lord.

PSALM 27:14 NLT

Patience is all about waiting things out. It's about holding on another moment longer. It means enduring hard times. As a younger person, you probably felt you couldn't possibly endure certain things, but the older you get, the more you realize that you can. If you just wait long enough, the tide always turns. Hold on. Your life will change. God's grace will rescue you.

Lord, help me to wait patiently for You. Help me to be brave
and courageous. Remind me that the tide does always
turn and that You will come through for me. Amen.

He's Waiting. . .

"The eyes of the LORD watch over those who do right,
and his ears are open to their prayers."

1 PETER 3:12 NLT

You don't have to try to get God's attention. He is watching you right now. His ear is tuned to your voice. All you need to do is speak, and He will hear you. Receive the gift of grace He gives to you through prayer. Tell God your thoughts, your feelings, your hopes, your joys. He's waiting to listen to you.

Father, what a comfort it is to know You are watching over me and that Your ears are always open to my prayers. Thank You for the gift of Your presence. Amen.

The Present Moment

"This day is sacred to our Lord."

NEHEMIAH 8:10 NIV

Sometimes we're in such a hurry to get to the future that we miss out on the present. God has gifts He wants to give you right now. Don't be so excited about tomorrow that you overlook the grace He's giving you today.

Heavenly Father, thank You for the gift of this moment.
Keep my eyes and heart focused on the here
and now, and immerse me in Your grace. Amen.

Near at Hand

Quiet down before G od, be prayerful before him.
PSALM 37:7 MSG

It's not easy to be quiet. Our world is loud, and the noise seeps into our hearts and minds. We feel restless and jumpy, on edge. God seems far away. But God is always near at hand, no matter how we feel. When we quiet our hearts, we will find Him there, patiently waiting, ready to show us His grace.

Lord, when my heart is restless and jumpy, remind me that You are near, waiting to comfort me with Your love. Quiet me with Your nearness. Show me Your grace. Amen.

Simply Love

But I am giving you a new command.
You must love each other, just as I have loved you.

JOHN 13:34 CEV

Christ doesn't ask us to point out others' faults. He doesn't require that we be the morality squad, focusing on all that is sinful in the world around us. Instead, He wants us to simply love, just as He loves us. When we do, the world will see God's grace shining in our lives.

Jesus, there is such simplicity in merely loving others with Your love. Help me to follow this new command and let the world see Your grace shining in my life. Amen.

Drawing Back the Curtains

But whenever someone turns to the Lord, the veil is taken away. . . . So all of us who have had that veil removed can see and reflect the glory of the Lord. And the Lord— who is the Spirit—makes us more and more like him as we are changed into his glorious image.

2 CORINTHIANS 3:16, 18 NLT

Sometimes we feel as though a thick, dark curtain hangs between us and God, hiding Him from our sight. But the Bible says that all we have to do is turn our hearts to the Lord and the curtain will be drawn back, letting God's glory and grace shine into our lives. When that happens, we can soak up the light, allowing it to renew our hearts and minds into the image of Christ.

Lord, thank You for removing the veil that hung between us. Turn my heart to You and draw me to Your light, renewing my heart and mind and making me more like Christ. Amen.

Mind, Body, Spirit. . .

I stretch myself out. I sleep.
Then I'm up again—rested, tall and steady.
PSALM 3:5 MSG

Rest is one of God's gifts to us, a gift we regularly need. In sleep, we are renewed, mind, body, and spirit. Don't turn away from this most natural and practical of gifts!

Father, the gift of sleep is a glorious thing. Help me not to resist this gift, and help me to recognize the necessity of being refreshed and renewed by hours of rest. Amen.

The Right People

The LORD God said, "It isn't good for the man to live alone. I need to make a suitable partner for him."

GENESIS 2:18 CEV

God understands that human beings need each other. His love comes to us through others. That is the way He designed us, and we can trust His grace to bring the right people along when we need them, the people who will banish our loneliness and share our lives.

God, thank You for creating me to live in harmony with other people. Thank You for showing me Your love through others. Help me to love them well. Amen.

Lifted Up

But those who trust in the LORD will find new strength.
They will soar high on wings like eagles. They will run
and not grow weary. They will walk and not faint.

ISAIAH 40:31 NLT

Do you ever have days when you ask yourself, "How much
further can I go? How much longer can I keep going like
this?" On days like that, you long to give up. You wish you
could just run away from the world and hide. Trust God's
grace to give you the strength you need, even then. Let Him
lift you up on eagle's wings.

Heavenly Father, I place my trust in You. Thank You for the
promise that I will soar high on eagle's wings. Give me rest
for my weariness and strength for the journey. Amen.

Scripture Index